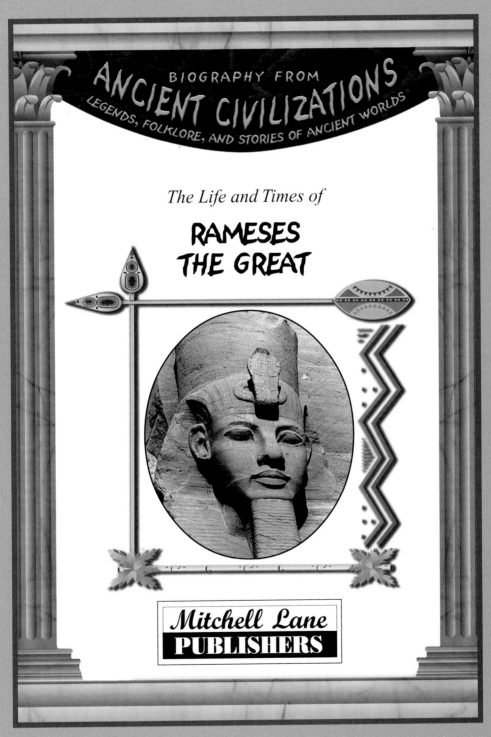

BIOGRAPHY FROM
ANCIENT CIVILIZATIONS
LEGENDS, FOLKLORE, AND STORIES OF ANCIENT WORLDS

The Life and Times of

RAMESES
THE GREAT

Mitchell Lane
PUBLISHERS

P.O. Box 196
Hockessin, Delaware 19707

BIOGRAPHY FROM
ANCIENT CIVILIZATIONS
LEGENDS, FOLKLORE, AND STORIES OF ANCIENT WORLDS

Titles in the Series

The Life and Times of:

Alexander the Great
Archimedes
Augustus Caesar
Buddha
Catherine the Great
Charlemagne
Cleopatra
Confucius
Constantine
Genghis Khan
Hammurabi
Homer
Joan of Arc
Julius Caesar
Marco Polo
Moses
Nero
Pericles
Rameses the Great
Socrates

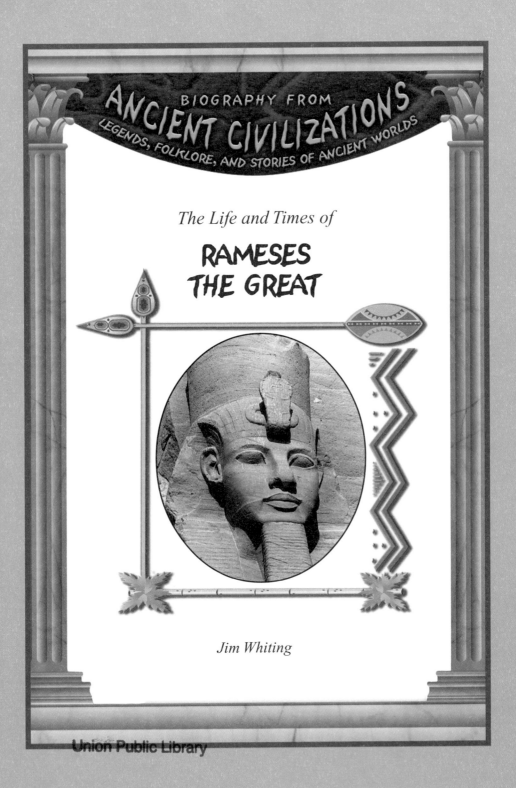

BIOGRAPHY FROM
ANCIENT CIVILIZATIONS
LEGENDS, FOLKLORE, AND STORIES OF ANCIENT WORLDS

The Life and Times of

RAMESES
THE GREAT

Jim Whiting

Mitchell Lane

PUBLISHERS

Printing   1   2   3   4   5   6   7   8

Library of Congress Cataloging-in-Publication Data

Whiting, Jim, 1943-
    The life and times of Rameses the Great / by Jim Whiting.
        p. cm. — (Biography from ancient civilizations)
    Includes bibliographical references and index.
    ISBN 1-58415-341-5 (library bound)
    1. Rameses II, King of Egypt—Juvenile literature. 2. Egypt—History—Nineteenth dynasty, ca. 1320–1200 B.C.—Juvenile literature. 3. Pharaohs—Biography—Juvenile literature. I. Title. II. Series.
DT88.W47 2005
932'.014—dc22

2004024605

ABOUT THE AUTHOR: Jim Whiting has been a journalist, writer, editor, and photographer for more than 20 years. In addition to a lengthy stint as publisher of *Northwest Runner* magazine, Mr. Whiting has contributed articles to the *Seattle Times*, *Conde Nast Traveler*, *Newsday*, and *Saturday Evening Post*. He has edited more than 100 Mitchell Lane titles in several series. A great lover of classical music and ancient history, he has written many books for young adults, including *The Life and Times of Irving Berlin* and *The Life and Times of Nero* (Mitchell Lane). He lives in Washington state with his wife and two teenage sons.

PHOTO CREDITS: Cover, pp. 1, 3, 10, 30, 33, 36, 39—Ancient Egypt Archives; p. 6—Artlex; pp. 8, 16—Corbis; p. 12—Utazas Webring; p. 14—Egypt Archive; p. 19—National Chiao Tung; p. 24—Art History; p. 34—Wakaba.jp; p. 41—Library of Congress.

PUBLISHER'S NOTE: This story is based on the author's extensive research, which he believes to be accurate. Documentation of such research is contained on page 47.

The internet sites referenced herein were active as of the publication date. Due to the fleeting nature of some web sites, we cannot guarantee they will all be active when you are reading this book.

BIOGRAPHY FROM
ANCIENT CIVILIZATIONS
LEGENDS, FOLKLORE, AND STORIES OF ANCIENT WORLDS

The Life and Times of

RAMESES THE GREAT

*For Your Information

This golden image is from the coffin of Tutankhamen, one of the most famous Egyptian pharaohs. He died while he was still a teenager.

CHAPTER
ONE

THE CURSE OF THE MUMMY?

On November 26, 1922, archaeologist Howard Carter could barely contain his excitement. He was standing just outside the sealed chamber that he believed contained the mummy and treasure of King Tut.

"King Tut" is the popular name of Tutankhamen (pronounced too-tang-KAH-mun), an obscure Egyptian pharaoh, or king, who died while he was still a teenager more than 3,300 years ago. As was the case with other pharaohs, Tutankhamen's body was mummified and then buried in an ornate tomb. A huge stash of gold, jewels, and other valuable objects was buried along with him for use in the afterlife.

Not surprisingly, the vast riches in the burial places of the pharaohs attracted the attention of grave robbers. Despite the prospect of severe penalties if they were captured, these robbers systematically plundered the tombs. When archaeologists began their excavations in Egypt in the late nineteenth century, they were disappointed that all the tombs they dug up had long since been looted of their treasures.

One of these archaeologists was Carter, an Englishman who arrived in Egypt in 1890. As he worked diligently during the succeeding years, he grew frustrated at the extent of the losses. Then he became convinced that one tomb hadn't fallen victim to grave

Lord Carnarvon (on the left), his daughter Lady Evelyn Herbert, and archaeologist Howard Carter stand just outside the entrance to the tomb of Tutankhamen.

robbers, that its treasure lay untouched. It was King Tut's. No one knew where it was, but Carter thought he could find it. His belief was so strong that he convinced an English nobleman named Lord Carnarvon to support him financially. After many years of failure, however, Lord Carnarvon got tired of pouring money into something that didn't seem to be going anywhere. He told Carter he was canceling the project. Carter begged for another year.

That was all the time he needed. Early in November 1922, he found a hidden door with the name *Tutankhamen* inscribed on it. He immediately sent word to Lord Carnarvon in England, and then waited for his patron to arrive. Now it was time to see if he was right.

Carter made a small opening, then lit a candle and leaned inside the chamber. It took a few moments for the candle to burn brightly enough so that Carter could see what lay inside. He gasped. He saw statues, furniture, jewelry. Nearly all of it was gleaming gold. Just as he had predicted, the tomb was packed with priceless treasures. One of the most impressive items was a series of three interlaid caskets. The innermost one, weighing more than a ton, was made of solid gold and contained the mummy of Tutankhamen.

A few months later, an American novelist named Marie Corelli wrote a letter to the *New York Times*. She claimed to own a copy of a book written many centuries earlier that said, "Death comes on wings to he who enters the tomb of a pharaoh."[1] She predicted that everyone who had entered the tomb of the young pharaoh would soon die. Only a handful of newspapers paid any attention to her views.

But a few days later, Lord Carnarvon died. A mosquito bite became infected and led to a fatal case of pneumonia. By chance, at the same time a British newspaper reporter was interviewing Sir Arthur Conan Doyle, the author of the Sherlock Holmes stories. The reporter mentioned Carnarvon's death and Corelli's letter to Doyle, who was a deep believer in spiritualism. That was all it took. The opinions of an obscure novelist could be easily dismissed. The opinions of an internationally famous writer were an entirely different matter.

"Conan Doyle was much struck by it and said that he believed the death was indeed the vengeance of the dead pharaoh," writes Egyptologist Christine El Mahdy. "On that day the idea of the curse became a fact, and the story made front-page news around the world. Details were added to embellish the tale. For example, at the time of Carnarvon's death, the lights had gone out in Cairo—a frequent occurrence even today—and this was taken as another sign that the ancient kings were punishing the violators of their peace. The words of the curse written by Marie Corelli now gained such an aura of authenticity that some newspapers declared the inscription had been found in the tomb itself."[2]

By this time, millions of moviegoers had seen films that featured mummies, one of the most popular subjects of this relatively new

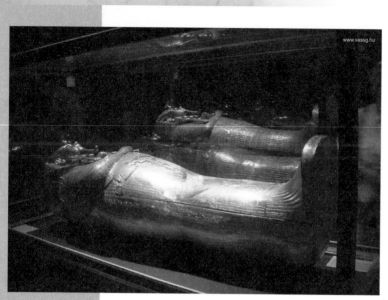
This solid gold casket holds the mummy of Tutankhamen.

addition to the entertainment industry. Many of these mummy movies were set in Egypt and involved conditions that somehow set off a curse. It was therefore easy for many people to believe that the opening of King Tut's tomb and the discovery of his mummy had set off a real-life curse.

The story gained credence as other people involved in the discovery of the tomb appeared to die of unnatural causes. Rumors began circulating. A cobra had supposedly eaten Carter's pet canary at the moment he had discovered the tomb. Carnarvon's favorite dog had howled at the moment of his master's death, then dropped dead—or so the story went. People claimed that Carter had suppressed a tablet that contained warning of a curse if anyone entered the tomb. There were reports of a wound on Tutankhamen's cheek—the same location where the mosquito had bitten Carnarvon.

Others were more skeptical about the existence of King Tut's curse. They pointed out that if anyone should have been a victim of the curse, it would have been Carter himself. Yet he lived to the age of sixty-six and died of natural causes. They also noted that Carnarvon had long been in ill health. It wouldn't have taken much to kill him, especially in the relatively unhygienic environment of Egypt in the early twentieth century. Many years later, after the furor about a possible curse had subsided, scientists began conducting experiments that might explain some of the untimely deaths of people connected with the discovery.

One theory was that dormant bacterial spores might have been responsible for at least some of the deaths. When fresh air came into the tomb, the theory ran, these spores would have become active and could have caused infections. Archaeologists now wear surgical masks and rubber gloves when they are dealing with mummies.

There is, however, no doubt about the value or the fascination of King Tut's treasure trove. It has circulated around the world in traveling exhibitions, always drawing huge crowds willing to endure lengthy waits to gaze in awe on these ancient artifacts. It is his treasure, rather than his accomplishments, that accounts for his fame.

King Tut isn't the only mummy to receive star treatment in recent years. In 1976, the mummy of Rameses II (RAM-uh-seez; the name is also spelled Ramesses and Ramses) was flown to France. When the airplane landed, Rameses' mummy was received with the full recognition accorded to the leader of a country: a band, a military honor guard, and a greeting from the French secretary of state.

Unlike King Tut, Rameses' reputation didn't have to be rescued from obscurity. The second-longest reigning pharaoh in the long history of Egypt, he was one of a handful of rulers throughout the entire world to have "The Great" added to his name.

Professor Nurel Din commented, "He was a great military man, he was a man of peace, he was the greatest builder in ancient Egypt, he had the biggest statue, he was the husband of a well-known lady, he had more children than any king of Egypt, he lived longer than any

This elaborately decorated chair is one of the priceless treasures taken from the tomb of Tutankhamen.

king of Egypt. Even nowadays he has the best-preserved mummy. . . . The biggest square in Egypt is called Rameses, the biggest street in Egypt is called Rameses, whenever you send statues of Rameses anywhere in the world, people line up to buy tickets. In ancient and modern times, there is no doubt that Rameses II is great."[3]

Hollywood has helped to perpetuate this aura of "greatness" by matching him with Moses, who according to the Bible led the Jewish people out of slavery in Egypt. One of the epic films during the silent film era was Cecil B. DeMille's *The Ten Commandments*, released in 1923. DeMille concluded his career in 1956 with a spectacular remake, which starred Charlton Heston as Moses and ran for nearly four hours. In 1998, DreamWorks made *The Prince of Egypt*, an animated film with an all-star cast. Rameses is a major character in all three films.

MOSES AND RAMESES

Moses

Both *The Ten Commandments* and *The Prince of Egypt* depict Moses and Rameses as friends when they are young men. Eventually loyalty to their respective people drives a wedge between them. Moses wants to lead his fellow Hebrews out of captivity. Rameses—who by this time has become pharaoh—objects. He needs their continued labor. After a series of plagues afflicts the Egyptians, Rameses changes his mind. He allows Moses to depart at the head of the Hebrews.

Then Rameses changes his mind again. He sends troops in pursuit of the Hebrews, who arrive at the Red Sea and appear to be trapped. Moses appeals to God, the Red Sea opens up, and the Hebrews escape into the desert on the far side. When the Egyptians try to follow, the sea rushes in to fill the opening, and they are all killed.

No one knows exactly when Moses lived, or the identity of the pharaoh at the time of the events described in Exodus, the Old Testament book that describes the Hebrews' flight from Egypt. It is likely that the Hebrews had been in Egypt for a considerable amount of time, perhaps as long as several centuries. For them, leaving Egypt was highly significant.

As author Bruce Feiler explains, "Exodus is more than an event, it's the seminal demonstration of how God involves himself in the daily lives of the Israelites, exercises control over other nations, and ultimately changes the course of history."[4]

Things were different for the Egyptians. According to the respected Egyptian scholar Joyce Tyldesley, "Most experts would agree that it [the pharaoh] must be Ramesses, with the Exodus far less dramatic and of far less significance to the Egyptians than the Bible would suggest, occurring some time during the first half of his reign. The Egyptian texts make no mention of a time of plagues and runaway workers, nor indeed of parting waters and drowned soldiers, but we would not expect them to; defeat, however minor, did not figure in Egypt's official history."[5]

The pharaoh Akhenaten, his statue shown here, made radical changes in Egyptian society. The primary one was forcing people to worship just one god.

CHAPTER
TWO

THE GIFT OF THE NILE

By the time Rameses was born, probably about 1304 B.C., Egypt already had a long history. Its civilization most likely began around 3150 B.C.—making Rameses' date of birth nearly as far removed from Egypt's beginning as our own era is from the birth of Jesus.

Not surprisingly, there were many changes during those nearly two thousand years. Fortunately for scholars, the Egyptians kept excellent records. The discovery of the Rosetta stone at the end of the eighteenth century allowed scholars to read these records. They established two methods of listing Egyptian history. One is by dynasties. A dynasty is a series of kings who are related by birth. Writing in the third century B.C., a Greek named Menthos identified thirty-one such dynasties. Some dynasties lasted longer than others, and certainly some were more important than others.

The other method involves grouping these dynasties into longer periods. According to historians, Egypt had three extensive epochs— each lasting several centuries—that were characterized by strong central governments. These are known as the Old Kingdom, the Middle Kingdom, and the New Kingdom. These three kingdoms were preceded by the Early Dynastic Period—when a shadowy ruler known as the Scorpion played a role in establishing the first dynasty—and

A scene on the Nile River, near Egypt's capital of Cairo dating back to the 1890s. It looks west toward the famous pyramids that are one of the country's primary tourist attractions.

three intermediate periods. There was also a so-called Late Period, in which Egypt had become so weakened that it was sometimes occupied by foreign powers. The final occupation came during the period that the Roman Empire was established. In 30 B.C., Egypt became a Roman province following the suicide of its famous queen, Cleopatra.

However, while scholars do agree on how these time periods are grouped, it has so far been impossible to nail down exact dates for the earliest times. Scholars sometimes disagree by a few years, sometimes by centuries—but the order of events is always the same.

Throughout all these changes, there was one thing that never changed: the Nile River. The world's longest river, it rises in central Africa and flows north to the Mediterranean Sea (see map on p. 24). Though it was possible to travel up and down the river on its banks, either on foot or on the back of a donkey or camel, the easiest way was by boat. The Nile was a boatman's dream. The current easily carried boats downriver. For the return trip upriver, most of the time the crew would raise a sail and allow the prevailing wind to do the work.

Even more important for Egypt's prosperity was what Greek historian Herodotus termed "the gift of the Nile." Every year between July and September, the river would be flooded and overflow its banks. The floodwaters carried millions of tons of valuable minerals that provided vital nutrients for the crops that fed the Egyptians. Farmers dug an intricate network of canals that carried the precious water to their land. This water was especially important because rain hardly ever fell in this area.

Nearly everyone in Egypt lived within a few miles of the river. The Egyptians had two names for their land. *Kmt*, or "Black Land," was the name for the fertile borders—usually just a few miles wide— of the river. *Dsrt*, or "Red Land," was the name of the surrounding, barren desert.

There was another division, into Upper and Lower Egypt. Lower Egypt began at modern Cairo, the point at which the Nile splits into several smaller flows that are known as the Delta and which enter the Mediterranean along an arc of nearly 150 miles. Upper Egypt stretched southward for hundreds of miles.

For nearly all of Egyptian history, there was another element that never changed. The people worshiped many gods, who regulated almost every aspect of their lives.

Soon after the beginning of his reign in 1379—more than 200 years after the beginning of the New Kingdom—the pharaoh Akhenaten (ah-kuh-NOT-'n) introduced a radical new concept. He declared that the sun god Aten (AH-tun) was the single god to worship, and he closed temples dedicated to all the other gods. He built a new city called Amarna, and unlike his predecessors, he spent nearly all his time there. So much time, in fact, that he ignored developments on the borders of the kingdom. Only about a century earlier, the so-called Napoleon of ancient Egypt—Thutmose III (thut-MOE-seh)—had pushed the border almost to the southern boundary of modern Turkey, capturing more than 350 cities and bringing many people under Egyptian control.

With Akhenaten paying little attention, these borders were being whittled away. By the time of his rule, the Egyptians' chief rivals were the Hittites, whose capital city of Hatti was located in modern Turkey.

The Hittites penetrated south and took over some lands in modern Syria that had previously belonged to Egypt. The Nubians, who lived along the Nile to the south of the Egyptians, also became restive.

When Akhenaten died after seventeen years of rule, he was succeeded by Tutankhaten (too-tang-KAT-'n), who was probably one of his sons. One of the new pharaoh's first acts was to change his name to Tutankhamen. The slight difference in spelling—changing the final *t* to an *m*—was important. It showed that Amun (AH-mun; his name is also spelled Amen), who before Akhenaten's accession had been the most important god, was replacing Aten and being restored to his previous importance. Tutankhamen also reopened the temples honoring the other gods.

The new pharaoh was young and healthy. So was his wife. It appeared as though Egypt would return to normal conditions. Tutankhamen seemed destined for a long rule, allowing plenty of time for his country to recover from the stresses and strains that had existed under Akhenaten.

Events soon proved otherwise. Tutankhamen died mysteriously when he was about eighteen. Some historians believe that he was poisoned by his chief adviser, Ay (EYE). The boy-king's widow sent a letter to the Hittite king, asking for a Hittite prince to marry her now that she was the widowed queen of Egypt. Though the king was suspicious of the offer, the chance to install a Hittite on the throne of Egypt was worth the risk. He sent one of his princes, but the young man was murdered before he could even reach Egypt. Having a foreigner become pharaoh was totally against Egyptian tradition. The killing further soured relations between the Hittites and the Egyptians.

Ay became pharaoh in place of Tutankhamen, but died after just four years. He was succeeded by Horemheb (HOOR-um-heb), a noted general, who restored the power and prestige of the Egyptian army. Because Horemheb didn't have a son, he selected an army officer

This scene depicts the pharaoh Horemheb worshipping Amun, one of ancient Egypt's most important gods.

named Pa-Ramessu, or Rameses, as his heir. While Rameses had proved himself as a good military commander, for Horemheb he had an even more appealing qualification. Rameses already had a son and a grandson who would be in line to inherit the throne. That would reduce the confusion and instability that had recently marked Egyptian life. Rameses I, as he became known, thus became the founder of the Nineteenth Dynasty.

Horemheb's judgment proved sound when Rameses died less than two years after taking over the throne. There was an orderly transition of power as he was succeeded by his son Seti (SET-ee). Seti immediately set out to restore his country's previous power by leading a series of successful military campaigns.

Seti was married to a woman named Tuya (TOO-yuh), who was also from the military class. They had a son who died in infancy, a daughter Tia, and then a second son. He was named Rameses II, after his grandfather.

Chapter THREE

From an early age, Seti made sure that his son was aware of his military responsibilities. As archaeologist Kent R. Weeks notes, "We know that Ramesses probably did accompany his father on military campaigns when he was five and six years old, but because of his age he was almost certainly an observer, judiciously placed out of harm's way, and not in the front lines commanding troops."[1]

Seti was also conscious of the need to establish Rameses as his heir. At the age of ten the boy was promoted to Eldest King's Son, giving him a princely status. He was also named commander in chief of the army, though this was purely an honorary title because Rameses was so young. Not long afterward, he received a more substantial appointment. Rameses was installed as regent, which meant that he had a voice in government.

Rameses clearly remembered the ceremony many years later.

"When my father appeared to the populace, I being just a youth in his embrace, he spoke [thus] concerning me:

" 'Cause him [Rameses] to appear as King, that I may see his beauty while I yet live!'

"So, he had the Chamberlains summoned, to set the crowns upon my brow. 'Place the Great Crown upon his head!',—so said he of me, while he yet was on earth—'he shall direct his land, he shall attend to [its affairs], he shall command the populace.' He spoke thus . . . because so great was the love for me within him.

"He furnished me with a household from the Royal Harim [harem], comparable with the 'beauties' of the Palace; he selected for me wives. . . ."[2]

As this quote shows, Rameses was already married even though he had barely entered his teens. It is likely that he had two wives at this time. They were Nefertari (neh-fur-TAH-ree)—who was the Chief Queen until her death in about 1255 and was one of ancient Egypt's most famous queens—and Istnofret (IST-noe-fret).

Seti made sure that Rameses learned practical matters for becoming king. Part of his education included active involvement in his military campaigns. Rameses was given a minor role in an early battle against the Libyans, who threatened the Nile Delta.

With his western flank secure, Seti turned his attention northward. He recaptured the northern kingdom of Amurru (in modern Lebanon) and Kadesh, a city of vital strategic importance because it controlled the easiest invasion route into modern Syria and beyond. Rameses was at his side as Seti extended Egypt's boundaries to the same extent they had been under Thutmose III.

Serving with the army, while exciting, took up only a couple of months each year, since most military campaigns in that era began in the spring and ended sometime during the summer. There was much else to learn about governing the kingdom. Part involved routine administration. Part involved traveling up and down the Nile on tours of inspection. Part involved honoring the numerous gods with elaborate festivals. And a major part involved overseeing fantastic feats of engineering. During the first year of his regency, Rameses supervised the construction of a large gold statue of his father. He also obtained permission to build a temple to the god Osiris not far from a huge one his father had already begun.

About the time that Rameses turned twenty, Seti decided that it was time for his son to take charge of a military campaign. Rameses led troops against the Nubians, who lived south of the Egyptians. Because there was little doubt about the outcome—the Egyptians were superior both in manpower and in the quality of their equipment—Rameses even took along his two eldest sons, age five and four. Keeping them well away from the actual fighting, he let them ride in their own little chariots so that they could believe they had helped their father win the battle. Soon afterward, he led an effort to rid the Nile Delta and the surrounding seas of pirates.

Chapter TWO

Then, probably in 1279, Seti suddenly died. The young prince was about to become the young pharaoh.

A pharaoh's death, especially one that was as unexpected as Seti's had been, would send shock waves throughout every level of Egyptian society. It could be regarded as a sign of the displeasure of the gods. To guard against this danger and to guarantee a successful reign for Rameses, the new pharaoh had to abide by a complicated series of rules and religious rituals.

Among the most important of these rituals was the lavish funeral for his father. Rameses must have been a little impatient as he waited the compulsory seventy days while the embalmers mummified his father's body, preparing it for Seti's journey into the afterlife. When the mummy was completed, the elaborate funeral parade proceeded up the Nile to the Valley of Kings. Located near Thebes, one of the capitals during the New Kingdom, the Valley of the Kings had become the traditional burial place of the pharaohs during that era. Under the careful oversight of priests, the body of the pharaoh was placed into its tomb, which was then sealed. No one watching the solemn ceremony could imagine that it would be sixty-seven years—the second-longest period in almost 2,000 years of Egyptian history—before there would be another funeral for a king.

Now in his mid-twenties, Rameses was ready to begin his rule. He must have felt very optimistic. He already had plenty of experience, both in government and in military matters. His kingdom was peaceful and prosperous.

One of the first orders of business was dealing with the Hittites. Helping his father conquer Kadesh had been a highlight of Rameses' teenage years. But Kadesh lay far from Egypt, close to the Hittites. Under an aggressive new emperor named Muwatallis (moo-wuh-TALL-us), the Hittites had regained control of the strategically important city. Amurru had also fallen to the Hittites.

For the ambitious young Rameses, that was an intolerable insult.

THE ROSETTA STONE

Egyptian scribes, the official writers of ancient Egypt, left behind extensive records. They used hieroglyphs, or picture writing, for those records. But the use of hieroglyphs ended about A.D. 400. After that, no one could understand them.

As Europeans began taking an interest in Egypt, they became frustrated because no one understood those hieroglyphs. They knew that the ancient writing contained invaluable information.

In 1798, French emperor Napoléon led an army to Egypt. The following year, a group of soldiers repairing a fort found a large black stone. It was covered with three different types of writing. On top was an inscription in hieroglyphs. A slightly later form of Egyptian writing was in the center. A Greek version was at the bottom. The stone was found in a town near the mouth of the Rashid, one of the branches of the Nile. Europeans called the river and the town Rosetta. The stone, therefore, became known as the Rosetta stone.

The discovery set off a great deal of excitement. It seemed obvious that each type of writing contained the same message. Translating the Greek part was easy, because many people in that era were familiar with ancient Greek. The challenge was to use this knowledge to decipher the other two inscriptions. Frenchman Jean-François Champollion was given the primary credit for "breaking the code." He began his efforts in 1808 when he was only eighteen. It took him fourteen years. His success made it possible for scholars to finally read the ancient hieroglyphs. This has vastly increased our knowledge of Egyptian history and the everyday lives of the people who lived many centuries ago.

Because the English defeated the French in several battles in Egypt after the stone's discovery, the English took possession of it. Today the Rosetta stone is on public display in the British Museum in London.

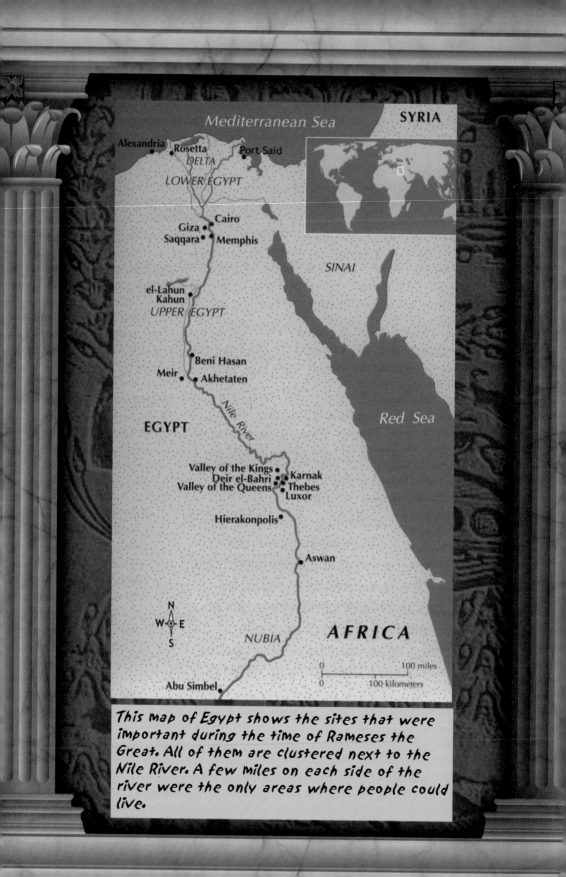

Mediterranean Sea

SYRIA

Alexandria
Rosetta
Port Said
DELTA
LOWER EGYPT

Giza
Cairo
Saqqara
Memphis

SINAI

el-Lahun
Kahun
UPPER EGYPT

Beni Hasan
Meir
Akhetaten

Nile River

EGYPT

Red Sea

Valley of the Kings
Deir el-Bahri
Karnak
Valley of the Queens
Thebes
Luxor

Hierakonpolis

Aswan

N
W E
S

NUBIA

AFRICA

0   100 miles
0   100 kilometers

Abu Simbel

This map of Egypt shows the sites that were important during the time of Rameses the Great. All of them are clustered next to the Nile River. A few miles on each side of the river were the only areas where people could live.

CHAPTER
THREE

THE BATTLE OF KADESH

Before he could take action against the Hittites, Rameses had a lot of other business to take care of. There were important positions in government and religion to be filled. More important for his already high sense of self-importance, he had decided to build a sprawling new city on the site of his father's summer palace. It lay in the Nile Delta, about halfway between the modern cities of Cairo and Port Said (see map on p. 24). He had no trouble finding a name for it: Pi-Ramesse A-nakhtu, or Domain of Ramesses-Great-of-Victories.

Construction began almost immediately. If Rameses had any doubts that the gods favored him, they were quickly dispelled. To build on such a massive scale required gold—lots of gold. There was gold in the desert, but without a reliable source of drinking water, it was impossible to sustain men long enough to mine it. Several pharaohs —including his father—had been unable to find water. Rameses told a group of noblemen that things would be different with him.

"Water has never been struck in this territory since the time of the God, as you say," he said. "But I shall open up a well there yielding water daily."[1]

He issued a set of detailed instructions to a party of diggers who set out into the arid wastes. Word soon came back. They had found water. It was possible for Rameses to begin mining the gold he wanted and needed so much. Once again, it seemed that he had shown that he had a magic touch.

Soon he decided it was time to turn to the Hittites. In the spring of 1275, he set out at the head of an army of about 20,000 men. According to tradition, they were split into four divisions of about 5,000 men. Each division was named after a god—Amun, Re (RAH), Ptah (p'TAH), and Seth—who would watch over and protect "his" division.

His goal was relatively modest: to return the kingdom of Amurru to Egyptian control. With no advance notice, the descent of Rameses' huge army resulted in a virtually bloodless conquest. The king of Amurru had to proclaim his loyalty to Rameses. To make sure that the king's loyalty didn't waver, Rameses left behind some of his soldiers when he returned home in triumph.

The following spring he went for the big prize: Kadesh. Again he set out with four full divisions. As he finally neared Kadesh, two men came up to him. They explained that they had deserted from the Hittite army and wanted to join Rameses' forces. Much more important, they told him that the Hittite army was more than 100 miles from Kadesh. They added that the Hittites were aware of the pharaoh's fierce reputation and were afraid to fight him.

Sensing Kadesh was ripe for the picking, Rameses rushed ahead with the Amun division. The other three divisions were strung out several miles behind him. That didn't seem important. Rameses felt confident that he could capture Kadesh before the Hittite army arrived.

Then one of his patrols appeared, dragging two Hittites with them. The unfortunate men had been captured and beaten severely. Under torture, they revealed a shocking fact. The two men he had met earlier were actually Hittite spies. They had been sent to provide disinformation, lulling Rameses into a false sense of security. The Hittites weren't a hundred miles away, cowering in fear. They were about two miles away, lurking just out of sight on the other side of Kadesh and eager to give battle. Rameses had blundered into an ambush.

Muwatallis had been surprised and embarrassed when Rameses had taken Amurru the previous year. Knowing that his rival would return, he had prepared a hostile reception by assembling an army even larger than the one Rameses led. He also understood psychological warfare. He knew that Rameses had a huge ego. The two spies had told Rameses exactly what he wanted to hear: that his reputation as a fighter had cast terror into his enemies. The flattered pharaoh hadn't made any effort to verify this intelligence. Now he had to pay the price.

Rameses was trapped on open ground with just a small portion of his army. He dispatched urgent messages to the other three divisions, ordering them to speed to his aid.

The Re division, the closest one, began covering the few miles that lay between it and the Amun division. Their haste spread them out. Without warning, hundreds of Hittite chariots splashed across the river that lay on the Egyptians' right flank, less than a mile away. The warriors in chariots hacked their way through the Re division, which in its disorganized condition put up little resistance. The remnants fled for the safety of the Amun division, with the chariots right behind them.

The safety they sought was a delusion. The men in the Amun were tired from their trek and had no time to prepare any defense. The Hittite charioteers began cutting up that division as well. Many of the panic-stricken men ran away. An Egyptian disaster seemed imminent as triumphant Hittites were closing in on Rameses himself. He was in danger of being captured.

When all seemed lost, Rameses leaped into his chariot. According to the official version of events, almost single-handedly he drove the Hittites back. A number of carvings depict his massive figure, bow and arrow in hand, towering over his rivals as he cuts them down.

While it is likely that Rameses did lead a courageous counterattack against his enemies, there were several other factors that saved the Egyptians. According to previous arrangements, the garrison he had left behind at Amurru would join him and help in the attack on Kadesh. At this critical moment, they made their appearance. The Hittites were forced to fight in two directions. Their horses and men would have become fatigued after several hours of intense combat in the hot sun. A number of the Hittite soldiers were also probably engaged in looting the Egyptian baggage train.

The heartened Egyptians—including many of the ones who had run away not long before—pushed the Hittites back across the river from which they had emerged earlier. According to one story, a Hittite prince swallowed so much water during his panic-stricken flight that he had to be held upside down to get rid of it all.

The Egyptians renewed the fighting the following day. After some initial successes, they met what proved to be an immovable object: more than 20,000 Hittite infantrymen. The battle ended indecisively. The Egyptians tallied up the enemy dead. They cut one hand off each corpse, threw the bloody trophies in a pile, and then counted them all.

Over the next few years, the Egyptians covered the walls of several temples with illustrations of the action. Royal scribes wrote down many details of the battle. Of course, the heroism of Rameses was always featured. The intention was to show how he had led the Egyptians to a great victory.

It is difficult to consider the battle of Kadesh as an Egyptian victory. While historians regard the battle as one of the most important in ancient times, its outcome was inconclusive. Even though the Egyptians were in possession of the field of battle at the end of the second day, they had not defeated the Hittites. Nor had they taken the city of Kadesh. Soon after the battle, they went back home. Kadesh remained Hittite. Never again would an Egyptian army try to capture it.

EGYPTIAN WARFARE

FYI
For Your Info

By the time of Rameses II, Egypt had made extensive conquests. It was necessary to keep the country's standing army to guard the country's expanded borders and to try to gain additional territory. The pharaoh was the commander-in-chief: He personally led troops during major battles.

The troops themselves came from several different sources. Some were volunteers. Others were conscripts, or draftees. A substantial number were foreign mercenaries, men who were paid well to join the Egyptians. Occasionally prisoners of war would decide to fight on behalf of their captors rather than becoming slaves.

Foot soldiers—who made up most of the army's personnel—were armed with a variety of weapons. These included heavy clubs, bows and arrows, lightweight throwing spears known as javelins, axes, knives, spears, swords, and even throwing sticks similar to boomerangs. Shields were their primary means of defense. Some had light body armor.

The "ultimate weapon" during this era was the chariot. Consisting of a wicker basket mounted on a pair of wheels and drawn by two horses, chariots had a two-man crew: a driver and a warrior. The warrior's primary armament was a bow and several quivers of arrows. He also had a long spear, several javelins, and a sword for close-range fighting.

Though most officers took pains to make sure that their men were well fed during campaigns, the life of a soldier could be difficult. Soldiers, as ever, faced the possibility of death in battle. Wounded men often succumbed to infections. When they weren't fighting, the troops had to endure extended marches, long hours, and heavy labor.

On the other hand, after serving for a certain period of time, soldiers were often rewarded with land. And victory in battle brought a more immediate bonus: loot. After a large enemy force was defeated, thousands of personal items belonging to the vanquished foes, many of considerable value, were distributed among the victors. A man who was recognized for individual bravery could expect a larger share of the bounty.

Many people consider the temple of Abu Simbel to be Rameses' most impressive building project. Each of the four massive statues depicts him. The tiny figures between his legs represent his wives and important sons.

CHAPTER
FOUR

THE MASTER BUILDER

The battle of Kadesh wasn't the final conflict between the Egyptians and the Hittites. Rameses led troops against them several more times. One of the more important campaigns was the siege of Dapur, a city not too far from Kadesh. Since Dapur was situated on a hill, the Egyptian soldiers had to attack from below. The Hittites easily dropped large stones on them and fired arrows down at them. Once again Rameses was depicted as a hero. According to the stories, he bravely appeared under the walls for several hours without his customary armor. The siege was eventually successful.

Even though the amounts of territory they lost were relatively insignificant, the Hittites were becoming more and more concerned about Egypt. The Assyrians, in modern Iraq, were pressing on their eastern border. In addition, King Muwatallis had died unexpectedly. His unpopular son Urhi-Teshub (UR-ee TESH-ub) succeeded him, but was eventually deposed by Muwatallis's brother Hattusilis III (hat-too-SILL-us). Urhi-Teshub fled to Egypt. Hattusilis demanded his return. Rameses refused to give him up. A renewal of hostilities appeared likely, with the Hittites trying to invade Egypt.

Then Hattusilis—fearing an Assyrian invasion on one side of his kingdom if he fought the Egyptians on the other—had a better idea. He proposed a peace treaty with Egypt in 1259. The two empires would pledge to respect each other's existing borders. Rameses must have had mixed feelings. If he agreed to the treaty, he would have to give up Kadesh and Amurru for good. On the other hand, the treaty guaranteed that he wouldn't have to worry about defending his borders. By then he was well into his forties. Going into battle may not have seemed as attractive as it had when he was a younger man. Perhaps he wanted to put his still-considerable energy into other areas. He agreed. What some historians regard as history's first peace treaty between two nations was signed. In an instant, bitter enemies became good friends.

So good, in fact, that more than a decade later a Hittite princess named Maathorneferure (ma-thorn-uh-fur-UHR-uh) became one of Rameses' brides. Seven years later, another princess—whose name is unknown—was sent south to become yet another of his wives.

These two Hittites were far from being the only wives that Rameses had. He lived so long that scholars estimate he may have had nearly a hundred wives, though they were not all of the same importance. The important ones—in addition to Nefertari and Istnofret—included at least three of his daughters. While marriages between a father and his daughters seem repellent to us today, in Rameses' time it was a well-established custom. In view of all the wives he had, it isn't surprising that historians estimate that he fathered between 100 and 200 children.

Having finally achieved peace with the Hittites and secured his northern border, Rameses could devote even more attention to his massive building campaigns. As noted Egyptian scholar and archaeologist Peter Clayton explains, the results were remarkable. "As a monument builder Ramesses II stands pre-eminent amongst the pharaohs of Egypt," he writes. "Although Khufu [KOO-foo] had

This is a representation of Queen Nefertari. She was Rameses' first wife and was considered to be Egypt's Chief Queen until her death at about the age of 50.

created the Great Pyramid, Ramesses' hand lay over the whole land. . . . His genuine building achievements are on a Herculean scale."[1]

His greatest architectural feat lay far to the south: the massive temple at Abu Simbel in Nubia. It was literally carved out of solid rock several hundred feet into the side of a hill that overlooked the Nile. In front are four massive statues of Rameses that stand nearly 70 feet tall. Images of his mother, of Queen Nefertari, and of several of his more important children reach barely to his mid-calf—showing their relative importance in his estimation. Inside are eight more statues of Rameses, each 30 feet high. The temple was designed so that the rising sun in mid-February and mid-October shone directly through the opening to cast light on the focal point of the interior: still another statue of Rameses, seated next to the god Amun.

The Aswan High Dam on the Nile created a lake that stretches to the south for hundreds of miles.

Abu Simbel was considered very important as a symbol of Egypt's past glories. When the Aswan High Dam on the Nile was designed during the 1960s, people realized it would create a huge artificial lake, completely submerging the temple. At a cost of millions of dollars, the temple and its statues were dismantled, moved to a nearby location safely above the new water level, and reassembled. Every year, it is a must-see for tourists.

BUILDING THE PYRAMIDS

FYI
For Your Info

When the pharaohs died, they wanted to lie in impressive structures that would show future generations how important they were. At first the pharaohs were buried in what were called mastabas, large rectangular buildings with sloping sides and flat roofs that were constructed of sun-dried mud bricks. These mastabas—and future tombs—were built on the western side of the Nile because that was where the sun disappeared every day.

Soon the pharaohs decided that mastabas weren't impressive enough. Imhotep (im-HOE-tep), an important official of a pharaoh named Djoser (whose name is also spelled Zoser, and whose reign began around 2670), had an idea. He constructed a square mastaba. Then he added five more mastabas, each smaller than the one directly underneath it, on top of the first one. This became known as the Step Pyramid; it soared nearly 200 feet into the air.

The most impressive pyramids were built in Giza, not far from modern Cairo, by three successive pharaohs—Khufu (also known as Cheops, pronounced KEE-ops), Khafre (KAF-ray), and Menkaure (mehn-KOO-ray). The pyramid built for Khufu—who reigned from about 2590 to 2565—was the largest, measuring nearly 500 feet high. More than two million blocks of solid stone, weighing between two tons and fifteen tons apiece, were used to construct it. According to some estimates, it contains enough blocks to build a wall entirely around France. As the pyramid rose higher, the stones had to be hauled up on ramps made of sand and mud. It was backbreaking work. It may have taken upwards of 100,000 workers twenty years to complete the project.

Pyramids continued to be built for several more centuries, but none approached the height of the Giza pyramids. Some were so poorly constructed that they collapsed under the immense pressures created by billions of pounds of stones.

The age of the pyramids ended when the capital of Egypt was moved several hundred miles south on the Nile. There was little flat ground on which to build. Instead, the tombs of the pharaohs were carved out of the cliffs on the river's western bank.

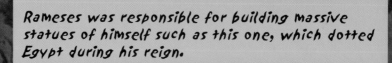
Rameses was responsible for building massive statues of himself such as this one, which dotted Egypt during his reign.

CHAPTER
FIVE

THE LEGACY OF RAMESES

To many people, it may have seemed that Rameses might live forever. More than three generations of Egyptians had grown up during his reign. His people had also witnessed many jubilee festivals, or *heb-seds*.

"The *heb-sed* . . . was originally a public ceremony of rebirth designed to reaffirm and re-enforce the aging king's powers after each successive thirty years of rule," explains Joyce Tyldesley. "By the New Kingdom it was accepted that the *sed*-festival would be celebrated after the first thirty years and then every three or four years thereafter."[1] It was a significant accomplishment for a pharaoh to enjoy a single *heb-sed*. Two of Rameses' predecessors survived long enough to celebrate three. Rameses obliterated that record by having fourteen.

These jubilees showed that he enjoyed absolute power during his reign. Absolute power over anything that he could control, that is. One of the forces he could not control was old age.

Tyldesley notes that in his later years, "All resemblance to the glorious victor of the battle of Kadesh had faded. The old king's face and neck were heavily lined—hardly surprising, given that he had lived for almost a century. . . . The severe arthritis that affected his hip, and the arteriosclerosis in his lower limbs, would have caused circulatory problems and would have prevented him from walking comfortably. . . .The king's teeth and gums were badly decayed and, in his final years, must have caused him constant pain."[2]

Finally the inevitable happened. In 1212 Rameses died. It must have been a momentous event. As Peter Clayton writes, "During his long reign of 67 years, everything was done on a grand scale. No other pharaoh constructed so many temples or erected so many colossal statues and obelisks. No other pharaoh sired so many children. Ramesses' 'victory' over the Hittites at Kadesh was celebrated in one of the most repeated Egyptian texts ever put on record. By the time he died, aged more than 90, he had set his stamp indelibly on the face of Egypt."[3]

One problem with Rameses' living so long was that many of his sons had died before him. His successor was Merneptah (mer-NEP-tah), the thirteenth son. He was probably nearly sixty when he ascended to the throne. His reign lasted just ten years, and he was succeeded by several weak pharaohs. Finally a governor named Setnakht (set-NOKT) took over the throne in 1185 and founded a new dynasty, the Twentieth. One measure of Rameses' continued importance was that Setnakht named his son after the great man. This pharaoh, Rameses III, is considered by most historians to be the last great pharaoh to occupy the throne of Egypt. He was followed by eight more Rameses, who collectively are known as the Ramessids and who ruled for another eighty years. By then, the power of Egypt was effectively broken. The era of the New Kingdom had ended. Never again would Egypt hold the same influence. Yet the country endured for more than a millennium, until it became a province of the Roman Empire in 30 B.C.

Though Rameses was dead, the adventures that involved him were not over. As was customary, his body was mummified and interred in an elaborate tomb in the Valley of the Kings, the final

The Valley of the Kings is the burial site for many pharaohs. It lies on the west bank of the Nile River, several hundred miles upriver from Cairo.

resting place of New Kingdom pharaohs. It wasn't destined for a peaceful rest.

By the end of the Twentieth Dynasty, tomb robbing had become common and extremely destructive. The mummies of Rameses and the other pharaohs in the Valley of the Kings were badly damaged by the looters. The priests of Amun gathered the mummies and repaired them as best they could. They also extracted most of the jewels that had originally been embedded in the linens. According to notes scrawled on his wrappings, as part of this preservation process Rameses was moved from his original tomb to his father's tomb, then to the tomb of a minor queen over the course of a few decades. Finally, along with many other mummies—now of virtually no interest to thieves because all of the valuables had been taken—Rameses was interred in the tomb of a high priest. The tomb became little more than a storage depot, holding the remains of many of Egypt's most powerful rulers. The site was soon forgotten. The mummy lay untouched for nearly 3,000 years, almost perfectly preserved in the dry desert heat. Then in 1871 the tomb was discovered—according to local legend, by a man looking for a lost goat. The man remained silent for ten years, and then word finally leaked out.

The Egyptian government realized the commercial potential of putting the mummies—especially one with so towering a reputation as Rameses—on public display. Despite the fascination felt by millions of onlookers as they gazed at Rameses, there was a downside.

"Rameses has spent much of the past century lying in the bottom half of a wooden coffin housed in a glass display case, a far from ideal environment for so fragile a specimen," notes Tyldesley. "With no means of controlling temperature, humidity or light, and no systematic monitoring of his body, Ramesses deteriorated. His skin cracked and was invaded both by bacteria and by over a hundred species of fungi."[4]

Salvation came from a somewhat unusual source. In 1836, the French had been given an obelisk that Rameses had erected at the city of Luxor. It was placed in a dominant position in Paris in the Place de la Concorde, a major civic gathering point.

In 1976, Paris played host to an extensive exhibition honoring Rameses. The French "invited" him to attend. His mummy was loaded onto an airplane and flown to Paris. After the plane landed and the welcoming ceremonies were over, Rameses spent the next eight months in French laboratories, undergoing state-of-the-art restoration in a custom-built lab. The wrappings on the mummy were removed and cleaned. His body was carefully examined. His skin was repaired with natural products such as turpentine and petroleum jelly, and then his body was rewrapped in the clean bandages and replaced in his wooden coffin base. For good measure, mummy and coffin were blasted with radiation to kill bacteria and fungi. Rameses was flown

Rameses' mummy as it exists today. Thousands of people view it every year in this temperature-controlled case.

back to Cairo and put back on public view in 1977 in a sealed case with a carefully controlled atmosphere.

Today, people can view the mummified remains of the man whom the English university professor of archaeology and classics K. A. Kitchen calls the "symbol of the proud majesty of Egypt through the ages."[5]

For many scholars and historians, the reign of Rameses marks one of the highest points in Egyptian history. Its power and prestige had expanded, its government had become even more efficient, and—of most importance to the people—it had enjoyed a long period of peace and prosperity. Certainly no other pharaoh left behind as many monuments as Rameses did.

As Bernadette Menu, an Egyptian scholar, writes so colorfully, "Ramesses remained the exemplar, in deeds and in memory dazzling and incomparable, like the sun at its zenith."[6]

FYI

For Your Info

How to Make a Mummy

The ancient Egyptians believed in an afterlife. To enjoy his second life, a pharaoh needed a physical body. Under normal circumstances, a pharaoh's corpse would begin to decay. Soon there would be nothing left. The answer was to preserve the body by making a mummy. By Rameses' time, the procedure had become fairly standardized.

First, embalmers laid the body on a table. They cut open the chest and removed the lungs, stomach, intestines, and liver and placed them in special containers called canopic jars. The kidneys were usually left behind. Frequently the heart would be removed, dried, and reinserted. The brain was a special case. Sometimes the back of the skull would be opened and the brain taken out that way. More often, the embalmers would insert a long needle with a hook through the nose and either scoop the brain out in little pieces or stir until it became a liquid. Then it could be drained through the nose.

The next step was to place the corpse inside a box that was filled with a type of white salt known as natron. Over a period of five or six weeks, the natron would draw out all the remaining moisture. As that happened, the skin took on a leathery appearance and the body shrank. The body was then coated with resin to make it waterproof.

During this lengthy process in the hot Egyptian climate, the corpse would begin to smell. Spices and other sweet-smelling substances were placed inside and on the corpse to counteract the odor.

After waterproofing, the wrapping began. It took two weeks or even longer. Hundreds of yards of linen would be used, with dozens of tightly wrapped layers that allowed the body to keep its shape. The name of the pharaoh was written at the ends of each layer of linen, enabling future historians to identify them.

When the wrappers were finished, the pharaoh's mummy would be placed inside a coffin that conformed to the shape of the body. In turn, this would be placed inside an even larger coffin. Accompanied by jewels, statues, and other artifacts, it was finally ready for the journey to the next life.

Chronology

All dates B.C. and approximate[1]

1304	Probable date of birth
1294	Is named Eldest King's Son
1290	Is named regent; likely date of marriages to Nefertari and Istnofret
1289	Participates in military campaign that captures Amurru and Kadesh
1279	Becomes pharaoh
1275	Undertakes first military campaign as pharaoh, in which he recaptures Amurru
1274	Battle of Kadesh
1269	Begins building temple of Abu Simbel
1259	Concludes peace treaty with Hittites
1258	Death of Tuya, his mother
1256	Dedicates Abu Simbel temples
1255	Chief Queen Nefertari dies
1250	Celebrates first jubilee festival
1246	Marries Hittite princess Maathorneferure
1245	Istnofret dies
1239	Marries a second Hittite princess
1225	Declares Merneptah as heir
1214	Celebrates his 14th, and final, jubilee festival
1212	Dies in August

BIOGRAPHY FROM

ANCIENT CIVILIZATIONS

LEGENDS, FOLKLORE, AND STORIES OF ANCIENT WORLDS

Timeline in History

All dates B.C. and approximate[1]

3100	The first Egyptian dynasty begins.
2700	The Early Dynastic Period ends and the Old Kingdom begins.
2590	The reign of Khufu, who built the Great Pyramid at Giza, begins.
2040	The Middle Kingdom begins.
1780	The Second Intermediate Period begins.
1570	The New Kingdom begins.
1504	Thutmose III begins his reign.
1450	Thutmose III dies.
1334	Tutankhamen (King Tut) becomes pharaoh.
1325	Tutankhamen dies under mysterious circumstances and is succeeded by Ay.
1321	Ay dies; Horemheb replaces him as pharaoh.
1293	Horemheb dies; Rameses I becomes pharaoh and begins the Nineteenth Dynasty.
1291	With the death of Rameses I, Seti I becomes the new pharaoh.
1279	Rameses II becomes pharaoh.
1260	Moses may have led the Jewish people out of Egypt at about this time.
1200	According to legend, the Trojan War begins.
1180	Rameses III becomes pharaoh.
1080	Rameses XI, the final pharaoh to bear the name and last king of the Twentieth Dynasty, dies.
1070	The New Kingdom ends and the Third Intermediate Period begins.
1000	Concerned about the continuing robberies of the pharaohs' tombs, a group of priests gathers the mummies and hides them.
525	The Late Period begins.
332	Alexander the Great founds the city of Alexandria on the Mediterranean coast; the city becomes a center of learning and culture.
304	The Ptolemaic Dynasty begins; it is Egypt's final dynasty.
30	With the death of Cleopatra, Egypt becomes a province of the Roman Empire.

Chapter Notes

CHAPTER ONE   THE CURSE OF THE MUMMY?
   1. Christine El Mahdy, *Mummies, Myth and Magic in Ancient Egypt* (New York: Thames and Hudson, 1989), p. 172.
   2. Ibid.
   3. Bruce Feiler, *Walking the Bible* (New York: HarperCollins, 2001), p. 175.
   4. Ibid., p. 174.
   5. Joyce Tyldesley, *Ramesses, Egypt's Greatest Pharaoh* (New York: Viking, 2000), p. 57.

CHAPTER TWO   THE GIFT OF THE NILE
   1. Kent R. Weeks, *The Lost Tomb* (New York: William Morrow and Company, 1998), p. 149.
   2. K. A. Kitchen, *Pharaoh Triumphant: The Life and Times of Ramesses II* (Warminster, England: Aris and Phillips Ltd., 1982), p. 27.

CHAPTER THREE   THE BATTLE OF KADESH
   1. K. A. Kitchen, *Pharaoh Triumphant: The Life and Times of Ramesses II* (Warminster, England: Aris and Phillips Ltd., 1982), p. 50.

CHAPTER FOUR   THE MASTER BUILDER
   1. Peter A. Clayton, *Chronicle of the Pharaohs* (New York: Thames and Hudson, 1994), p. 153.

CHAPTER FIVE   THE LEGACY OF RAMESES
   1. Joyce Tyldesley, *Ramesses, Egypt's Greatest Pharaoh* (New York: Viking, 2000), p. 157.
   2. Ibid., p. 15.
   3. Peter A. Clayton, *Chronicle of the Pharaohs* (New York: Thames and Hudson, 1994), p. 146.
   4. Tyldesley, p. 206.
   5. K. A. Kitchen, *Pharaoh Triumphant: The Life and Times of Ramesses II* (Warminster, England: Aris and Phillips Ltd., 1982), p. 237.
   6. Bernadette Menu, *Ramesses II: Greatest of the Pharaohs*, translated by Laurel Hirsch (New York: Harry Abrams, 1998), pp. 126–27.

CHRONOLOGY and TIMELINE IN HISTORY
   1. Peter A. Clayton, *Chronicle of the Pharaohs* (New York: Thames and Hudson, 1994), p. 153.

Glossary

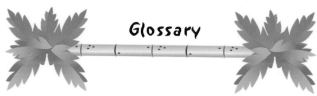

aberration	(a-buh-RAY-shun)—something that is different from the usual or normal way.
archaeologist	(ar-key-AH-luh-jist)—a person who studies previous civilizations.
conscript	(KON-script)—someone who is forced to join an army.
dormant	(DOOR-munt)—a state of temporary inactivity.
excavation	(ek-skuh-VAY-shun)—the process of digging, especially when it is done to uncover something.
harem	(HAIR-um)—the portion of a dwelling limited to women; also, a group of women associated with one man.
Herculean	(her-kyuh-LEE-un)—extraordinarily large, strong, or difficult.
hieroglyphic	(hie-ruh-GLIH-fick)—a system of writing that uses pictures rather than letters for words.
obelisk	(AH-buh-lisk)—a four-sided pillar that tapers as it rises and has a pyramid at the top.
patron	(PAY-trun)—a person who provides financial support for scientific or artistic work.
pyramid	(PIR-uh-mid)—a structure with a square base and triangular-shaped walls that come to a point at the top. Ancient Egyptian pyramids were used to entomb important people.
regent	(REE-jent)—a person who rules or governs.
restive	(RES-tive)—restless, nervous.
spiritualism	(spir-i-chew-wuh-IL-izm)—a belief that the dead can communicate with the living and have an effect on them.
spore	(SPOR)—a primitive life-form, often one-celled, that can develop into a new individual.
zenith	(ZEE-nith)—the highest point.

For Further Reading

For Young Adults

Cottrell, Leonard. *The Warrior Pharaohs*. New York: G.P. Putnam's Sons, 1969.

Morley, Jacqueline. *An Egyptian Pyramid*. New York: Peter Bedrick Books, 1991.

Perl, Lila. *Mummies, Tombs, and Treasure: Secrets of Ancient Egypt*. New York: Clarion Books, 1987.

Tiano, Oliver. *Ramses II and Egypt*. New York: Henry Holt and Company, 1995.

Works Consulted

Asimov, Isaac. *The Egyptians*. Boston: Houghton Mifflin Company, 1967.

Clayton, Peter A. *Chronicle of the Pharaohs*. New York: Thames and Hudson, 1994.

El Mahdy, Christine. *Mummies, Myth and Magic in Ancient Egypt*. New York: Thames and Hudson, 1989.

Feiler, Bruce. *Walking the Bible*. New York: HarperCollins, 2001.

Kitchen, K. A. *Pharaoh Triumphant: The Life and Times of Ramesses II*. Warminster, England: Aris and Phillips Ltd., 1982.

Menu, Bernadette. *Ramesses II: Greatest of the Pharaohs*. Translated by Laurel Hirsch. New York: Harry Abrams, 1998.

Montet, Pierre. *Everyday Life in Egypt in the Days of Ramesses the Great*. Translated by A. R. Maxwell and Margaret S. Drower. Philadelphia: University of Pennsylvania Press, 1981.

Tyldesley, Joyce. *Ramesses, Egypt's Greatest Pharaoh*. New York: Viking, 2000.

Weeks, Kent R. *The Lost Tomb*. New York: William Morrow and Company, 1998.

On the Internet

The American University in Cairo. Mummy Movies.
http://www.aucegypt.edu/academic/anth/anth400/mummy_movies.htm

Egyptian Monuments. "Temple of Rameses II."
http://www.egyptsites.co.uk/upper/luxorwest/temples/rameses2/rameses2.html

Egypt: Rulers, Kings, Pharaohs of Ancient Egypt. "Ramesses II."
http://www.touregypt.net/19dyn03.htm

PBS. Egypt's Golden Empire.
http://www.pbs.org/empires/egypt/

Ray, John. BBC. Egyptians. "Ramesses the Great."
http://www.bbc.co.uk/history/ancient/egyptians/ramesses_01.shtml

Stratos, Anita. Tour Egypt Feature: "The Evolution of Warfare, Part I."
http://www.touregypt.net/featurestories/war.htm

The UnMuseum. Howard Carter and the "Curse of the Mummy."
http://www.unmuseum.org/mummy.htm

Index